When the Catfish Had Ticks

When the Catfish Had Ticks

Texas Drought Humor

by

Rana Williamson

EAKIN PRESS ★ AUSTIN, TEXAS

FIRST EDITION

Published in the United States of America
By Eakin Press
A Division of Sunbelt Media, Inc.
P.O. Box 90159
Austin, TX 78709

2 3 4 5 6 7 8 9

ISBN 1-57168-159-0

Library of Congress Cataloging-in-Publication Data

When the catfish had ticks : Texas drought humor / [compiled] by Rana
   K. Williamson.
        p.   cm.
     ISBN 1-57168-159-0 (alk. paper)
      1. Texas--Humor. 3. Droughts--Texas-Humor   I. Williamson, Rana
   K.
   PN6231.T56W47   1997
   818'.540208--DC21   97-4267
                                                             CIP

To my father,
Loyd V. Williamson
(1921-1996).
He gave me the gift
of his humor.

Contents

Preface

A Texas rancher died and began his journey in the afterlife. His path to the Pearly Gates wound through a dry, parched land. When he reached his destination he said to the attendant, "Saint Peter, this looks just like Texas." The gatekeeper answered with a smile, "I'm not Saint Peter and you don't know where you're at!"[1]

I began to encounter stories like this while working on my master's and doctoral degrees at Southwest Texas State University and Texas Christian University respectively. In compiling a history of the 1950s drought, I discovered that hell moved to Texas in 1950 for a seven-year stay. The demon in charge, drought, was an old enemy in a cyclical, meteorological struggle dating back to the fifteenth century when an early occurrence destroyed the Antelope Creek Focus, a native culture on the Canadian River. Between 1891 and 1951, drought visited Texas eight times, but never for more than three years. In the fifties, however, the lethal combination of severity and duration drove agricultural debt past the $3 billion mark and necessitated $61.8 million in federal aid. As the crisis forced Texans to endure distasteful realities, they fought back psychologically by drawing on an oral tradition of black, "gallows" humor as a coping mechanism.[2]

Such a tradition, transmitted verbally from one generation to the next, tends to become less pronounced as a culture becomes increasingly literate and technologically oriented. In Texas, however, such drought-related material is alive and well, as is drought, judging from the hot summer of 1994. Oral historians recognize such storytelling as a valuable means of communicating historical experience, a fact borne out by the repeated submission to this book of a joke whose origin can be traced as far back as 1889.[3]

In working with drought jokes, I discovered that by holding up to ridicule the agents of their anxiety and frustration, Texans made them seem less formidable. Jokes became a source of temporary relief from the pressures generated by drought. Listeners understood the desperation in the words of the Big Spring banker who said, "If it don't rain pretty soon, looks like I'm gonna have to rob a bank." But when his friend replied, "If it don't rain pretty soon, looks like I've already robbed a bank," the laughter made debt a little less threatening and painful if only for a moment.[4]

Many of the anecdotes are time-worn. One story, dating back to 1919, featured two ranchmen discussing the serious lack of rain. "My cattle are so thin," said one, "that by using carbon paper, I can brand two at a time." In 1887 a man narrowly escaped a comical arrest in Anson. On a Monday morning passers-by spotted J.P. Cole walking down the street with a slicker draped over his arm. In the middle of a long dry spell, the sight attracted considerable attention. It offended S.C. Hines, who hastened to the sheriff's office and demanded Cole's arrest for "unlawfully carrying a slicker against the peace and dignity, dampness and future prospects of rain in the free state of Jones."[5]

But whether new or old, these anecdotes illustrate a simple principle. In a situation where crying will not help, laughing cannot hurt. In fact, laughter helps to diffuse tension and redirect harmful impulses into more constructive channels. In this manner, humor acts as a subconscious defense mechanism. It allows the body and the mind to withstand external threats and to cope with anxiety.[6]

As a by-product of drought, humor rounds out a sort of "drought mentality" characterized by the faith that rain will return and the determination to wait for that day. Obviously, then, the term "humor" applies to a subjective and exclusive body of material. When distinctive segments of society develop distinctive jokes, the punchlines often fall flat for outsiders. The boundaries of this understanding may be cultural, regional, professional, racial, sexual, or, as in the case of drought, circumstantial. As a result, however, humor common to a particular group can offer revealing insight into that group's values and concerns.[7]

Consider the story of the soldier who lost his hand in battle. A friend visited him in the hospital and asked about the injury. The soldier replied, "I decided to take the advice of the Yellow Pages — 'Let your fingers do the walking.'" To listeners who have not participated in or been wounded in battle, the joke seems grisly. They have difficulty finding, much less appreciating, its humor.[8]

By the same token, individuals outside the ranching community could hardly comprehend the irony in the experience of the man who bought three goats in 1954. He put the animals in a barrel and welded the top down to insure their safety. A week later he checked on them and found one sick, one dead and one gone. This testament to the perils of goat ownership reveals the low opinion ranchers held for the animals. It was only with reluctance and out of necessity that goat raising became widespread in Texas in the fifties, despite the benefits to be had from the relatively stable mohair market.[9]

This cynical and self-deprecating humor runs hand in hand with the western tradition of storytelling common to the "cowboy" culture. To these men, exaggerating really meant minimizing the rough and harsh quality of their lives and environment.

A typical tall-tale designed to make light of changeable Texas weather featured a cowboy riding along in blistering summer heat "hotter'n Satan in long handles." He turned around to find a "blizzard whizzin' in" just behind him. Putting the spurs to his horse, he tried to outrun the snow storm. When he reached the barn back at the ranch and began to unsaddle his horse, he discovered something peculiar about the animal. "Danged if . . . [he] didn't find its forequarters plum' foamy with sweat and its hindquarters frozen solid with ice . . . ."[10]

In the fifties the stubborn weather provided ample material for humorous jabs. Promising clouds often formed, only to offer a few meager drops before dispersing. Normally, annual rainfall ranges from 56 inches and above in East Texas to eight and below in the west near El Paso. At the drought's lowest point, 1956, overall average precipitation dipped to 16.20 inches and regional totals fell proportionately. While teasing sprinkles never produced enough moisture to offset the staggering deficiencies, they did prompt optimistic ranchers to brag about the five-inch rain they received — the drops were five inches apart.[11]

In these pages you will find "so dry" lines, appeals to the Almighty, ludicrous one-liners, and the viewpoint of children looking out at a confusing adult problem. There are tall weather tales and attempts at prediction and the dangers of real estate transactions in the Lone Star State. Texans have commented on the relevance of rain and water in every area of their daily lives, from the cowpen to the delivery room. They found uses for the deep cracks in the earth and sheltered confused catfish and frogs who never learned to swim. They battled dust and wind, low livestock prices and withered crops. But above all, they laughed when they could and they kept praying for rain. It's not a bad strategy.

Rana Williamson

It's So Dry . . .

. . . the jackrabbits are carrying canteens.

— **Pete McDonald, Plainview, J. D. Babin, Three Rivers, and Marvin L. Doss, Odessa, Texas**

. . . I saw two trees fighting over a dog.

— **David Hunt, Dallas, Texas**

. . . the cows are giving evaporated milk, and the chickens just plucked themselves to escape the heat.

— **Don Worcester, Weatherford, Texas**

. . . I saw an armadillo hitchhiking to Arizona.

— **Ken Francis, Abilene, Texas**

1

. . . the piss-ants can't.

— F.N. (Doc) Carter, San Angelo, Texas

. . . a grass widow wouldn't even take root.

— E.L. Odom, Baird, Texas

. . . I'm gonna stop buying toilet paper and just hang up a feather duster in the bathroom.

— Mark T. Beechie, Thornton, Texas

. . . I had to vacuum my post holes four times before I could get the poles in.

— Ken Francis, Abilene, Texas

. . . we have to soak the pigs before they'll hold slop.

— Pete McDonald, Plainview, Texas

. . . old farmers who chewed or dipped had to prime themselves to spit.

— **Glenna Cavanaugh, Garland, Texas**

. . . in Jones County the trees started chasing the dogs.

— **F.N. (Doc) Carter, San Angelo, Texas.**

. . . I saw a creek tracking down a rain cloud.

— **Ken Francis, Abilene, Texas**

. . . we had to run the well through the wringer on the washing machine to get water to cook with.

— **Glenna Cavanaugh, Garland, Texas**

. . . if a truck went by with a dog in the back, all the trees would lean towards the road and hope.

— **Sam Kelly, Jr., Harrold, Texas**

. . . we didn't dig foundations, we just waited for the ground to crack and filled it with cement.

— Ken Francis, Abilene, Texas

. . . and so hot the corn popped in the fields and the cows thought it was snow and froze to death.

— Glenna Cavanaugh, Garland, Texas

. . . it's drier than a grass widow's nipple.

— George Gawldin, Archer City, Texas

. . . I couldn't get the dust out of the postholes.

— Ken Francis, Abilene, Texas

. . . and our corn was so poor, Mama fixed corn on the cob for supper and Papa ate fourteen acres all by himself.

— W. H. Bodenhamer, Brady, Texas

. . . the weeping willows can't, they just look despondent.

— John Igo, San Antonio, Texas

. . . the catfish came up to the well to get a drink.

— Glenna Cavanaugh, Garland, Texas

. . . and hot we had to take down the barbed wire fences to get a breeze.

— Micki Zerbe, Gun Barrel City, Texas

. . . we had to import dogs for the sand fleas.

— John Igo, San Antonio, Texas

. . . I've got bullfrogs three years old that ain't even been wet.

— George Richie, Dallas, Texas

. . . I found a 61-pound catfish in the Pecos River at Horse Head Crossing near McCamey that had never learned how to swim.

— Jack W. Barltett, Ferris Texas

. . . we pumped the wells dry, pulled up the holes, and cut 'em in three-foot lengths for sale as post holes.

— **John Igo, San Antonio, Texas**

. . . and hot I saw a dog chasing a rabbit, and they were both walking.

— **Paul Bishop, Big Spring, Texas**

. . . that when you spit, it evaporates before it hits the ground.

— **Dr. J. Vernon McKay, Lamesa, Texas**

. . . a fellow caught a catfish that had ticks on it.

— **Edith Ferguson, Henrietta, Texas**

. . . you've got to sneeze to bring the relative humidity up to zero.

— **L. E. Howard, Jr., Dallas, Texas**

. . . the other day I saw a mockingbird trying to pull a worm out of the ground with a pot holder.

— **Inez Sport, Childress, Texas**

Divine Intervention

A "drouthed-out" stockman reported to the Pearly Gates and announced, "I'm Jasper Mulligan from Pecos County."

St. Peter consulted his book and said, "I'm awful sorry, but with a record like this . . . I'll have to send you down to Hell."

Mulligan shrugged and said, "Well, at least that's some improvement."

— **Elmer Kelton,** *The Time It Never Rained*, **195**

In 1889 Coleman County stockmen, beset by drought and a troubled economy, persuaded an elderly gentleman to lead them in prayer. As the men bowed their heads, he attempted to intercede with God. "Oh, Lord, give us help, give us barrels of flour, barrels of sugar, barrels of coffee, barrels of chile pepper . . ."

At that point, a neighbor jabbed him in the ribs and whispered, "Jim, dry as it's been, that's away to hell too much chile pepper."

— **"Just What's Needed, Lord,"** *Sheep and Goat Raiser*
(April 1954): 48

During a drought, the preacher suggested the community come together to pray for rain. A skeptic in his congregation said, "Go ahead if you want to, parson, but prayin' ain't gonna do you a damn bit of good unless the wind's outta the east."

— **Boyce House,** *I Give You Texas*, **6**

Different denominations suffered in different ways. In 1889 the *Taylor County News* reported a June so dry,

> the fish in the creeks are carrying toadstools for parasols . . . [and the] Baptists and Campbellites are beginning to favor baptism by sprinkling, and they have quit turning their noses up at Presbyterians . . . .

— **Quoted in William C. Holden, "West Texas Droughts,"**
Southwestern Historical Quarterly **32 (October 1928): 109**

One old-timer claimed things were so dry in his neck of the woods that the Baptists only sprinkled and the Methodists just used a damp cloth.

— **Don Worcester, Weatherford, Texas**

OR

. . . the Methodists were giving out promissory notes.

— **J.D. Babin, Three Rivers, Texas**

OR

. . . the Presbyterians were giving out rainchecks.

— Jerline K. Oakes, Sebastian, Texas

OR

. . . the Church of Christ went to pouring, the Methodists sprinkling, and the Presbyterians dry-cleaning.

— C. Randolph Coney, Ph.D., South Padre Island, Texas

Some Texans in the fifties didn't know exactly where to direct their prayers. Like many families on the Edwards Plateau, the Billy Allens of Kimble County listened to Henry Howell's farm and ranch program on radio WOAI, San Antonio, every morning at 6 o'clock. When the show ended, Billy would pick up his coffee and walk out to the yard, hoping to see some sign of rain.

One morning his little son, Tom, followed his father outside. They stood silently for a few minutes, hands on their hips, staring up at the clear sky. Then Tom solemnly asked, "Daddy, when are God and Henry Howell gonna let it rain?"

— Margaret Allen, Junction, Texas

10

"Get much rain out your place last week?"
"Naw, no mor'n a Methodist shower."

— Donald Chain Black, *Handy as Hip Pockets on a Hog: The Colorful Language of the American Southwest*, 42

The drought of 1925 hit hard on the Kirkland Ranch near Axtell in Central Texas. The stock tanks and wells dried up, and in the sun-scorched pastures the cows were down to hide and bone on a diet of mesquite beans. Two cattlemen met one morning along a dusty road and began talking about the weather.

"I was at church Sunday night," said one man, "and the preacher says he wants everyone to come to prayer meetings on Wednesday nights and pray for rain and them that can't come should pray at home."

"You reckon that'll help?"

"It sure as hell can't make things no worse."

"Well, then, why wait until Wednesday night? Why don't we start praying right here and now? You start off."

They dismounted, tied their horses, and removed their hats. In the scant shade of a scrub oak, the man began, "Lord, our pastures is burnt up, our water is all gone, and our cattle are dying. Don't bother with sending us no little shower. What we need is a rain that will make the jackrabbits run for the high ground and the turkeys take to the trees. Send us a stump-mover and a gully-washer . . ."

His friend broke in heatedly, "Now hold on just a minute! Don't listen to this feller, Lord. That's jist too damn much rain!"

— B.R. Thomas, Leroy, Texas

11

After a five-year drought, a cowboy prayed for rain, and sure enough, in about half an hour a shower came up. He turned to his buddy, very pleased with himself, and said, "If it don't rain in another five years, I'll pray again."

— F.N. (Doc) Carter, San Angelo, Texas

A Texan phoned the Weather Bureau to request information. "When in the hell are we gonna get some rain?"

"Sir, it really doesn't look very good right now. Everything is in the hands of God."

"You mean it's as bad as that? I reckon we're done for."

— Charles Brucks, Jr., Orlando, Florida

A man traveling alone across West Texas in a single-engine aircraft ran out of fuel and crashed. The soft sand and sage brush cushioned the landing enough that he escaped serious injury, but when he crawled out of the wreck he was dazed and confused.

As he stood up, he looked around and said, "Lord, I sure wish I had repented back at that last tent revival meeting 'cause this place is worse than the preacher said."

— Chuck Ferris, Denton, Texas

A West Texas farmer displayed an unconcerned attitude during a discussion of the drought and grasshopper infestation.

When his friend asked him why he was being so nonchalant, he said, "Well, I gave my farm to the Lord years ago, and if He wants to run grasshoppers on it, that's his business."

— **Jerry J. Hosek, D.V.M., Dallas, Texas**

In the thirties times were hard for everybody. In Shiro, Texas, the crops were withering in the fields. A group of men had gathered to discuss and cuss the government and the weather.

Hop Henderson spoke up and said, "You know, I guess the Lord is a pretty good feller, but he don't know a damn thing about farming."

— **Cornell Oliphant, Huntsville, Texas**

One-liners

Texans claim to live in the land of the five-inch rain — the drops are five inches apart.

— **Dean Chenoweth and Elmer Kelton, "Texas Dry Humor,"** *Reader's Digest* **(March 1953): 72**

A hen caught in a Panhandle dust storm had to lay the same egg half a dozen times.

This year the crops are so bad the crows have to lie on their stomachs to steal corn.

Round here we've had pet ducks and frogs fall into buckets of water and drown.

— **Don Worcester, Weatherford, Texas**

There's an Odessa oilman who needs water so badly for his drilling rig, he's offering to trade oil for it, barrel for barrel.

— Walter Prescott Webb, "Billion Dollar Cure for Texas Drought," *Harper's* (December 1953):73

Out in West Texas a cowboy was struck by a drop of rain, and the shock was so great it took two buckets of sand to revive him.

— House, *I Give You Texas*, 10

One steer can raise more dust than three Texas rains can lay.

— "Foxtail Johnson Objects," *Sheep and Goat Raiser* (March 1954): 28

Yes sir, grass has got so thin in my country that a cow's got to graze in a lope to stay ahead of starvation.

— Elmer Kelton, *The Time It Never Rained*, 195

It's so hot, we're feeding the hens chipped ice so they won't lay hard-boiled eggs.

— James V. White, Fort Worth, Texas

A farmer complained, "It's so dry, my cotton is smaller than it was when it was little."

— Juil E. Reid, Stanton, Texas

"Trading Post" radio ad in the 1950s: "Rain gauge for sale. Cheap. Slightly used."

— Dale Thompson, San Angelo, Texas

When is it gonna rain? At the end of this long dry spell.

— Dr. J. Vernon McKay, Lamesa, Texas

West Texas is so flat, all you have to do to see the whole thing is stand on a stump and turn around.

— Ruth Moye, San Antonio, Texas

If it doesn't rain when we need it, we will surely need it when it rains.

— George Gawldin, Archer City, Texas

In the fifties, fishermen had to take water with'em in the boat in case the river needed priming.

— Ken Francis, Abilene, Texas

Children of the Drought

In the fifties a father lamented, "I wish it would rain — not for my sake because I've seen it rain, but on account of my seven-year-old boy."

— Chariton, *Texas Wit and Wisdom*, 37. Another real favorite, with ten entries. Thanks to each.

Three Texans paced the floor of the maternity ward waiting for their children be delivered. After a while the nurse came into the room and showed the East Texas cotton farmer his ten-pound son. Another hour passed and she returned with the South Texas onion grower's nine-pound boy.

After what seemed like an eternity, the nurse finally walked in carrying the West Texas sheepman's five-pound baby daugher. The man was overcome with joy and gratefully accepted the congratulations of his new friends.

The cotton farmer couldn't keep from saying, "She's a beautiful little girl, but she's awful little. Why are you so happy?"

"Well, sure I'm happy," exclaimed the sheepman,

all grins. "It's been so dry in West Texas I'm just darned glad to save the seed."

— "Saving the Seed," *Sheep and Goat Raiser* (February 1953): 7

First grade students entering Goldsmith Elementary School in the fifties struggled with a readiness test that included the question, "Does it rain at night?" All the kids answered, "No." One teacher protested in their defense. The question just wasn't a fair one to ask little West Texas kids in the middle of a drought.

— Nicholas Banner, Odessa, Texas

One mother said to another, "My little Jimmy still believes in Santa Claus."

Her friend exclaimed, "So what! My Johnny still believes in rain."

— Ira Anderson, Jr., Tyler, Texas

Southeast of Pecos at the now-vanished site of Panama, Texas, a cowboy rode by one day to find the teacher standing on the school roof with a bucket.

"What in the hell are you doing, woman?" he called out.

"I'm going to pour this water on the roof and let it run off so I can show these kids what rain looks like."

— Tom Erskine, *Thirty Years West of the Pecos*, 35, sent by Fariss Murphy, Pecos, Texas

Carolyn McGuire was born in 1951. The only place she ever saw water produced was out at the windmill. When she was three or four years old, it finally rained some one afternoon. As she stood at the window watching, she called out, "Oooh! Mommie, it's windmilling outside."

— Betty Murr Norton, Junction, Texas

Another little four-year-old girl in Amarillo, confronted with a similarly inexplicable rain, ran into the house crying, "Mommy, I didn't turn the sprinkler on! I didn't turn the sprinkler on!"

— Ozella Parsons Plummer, Danbury, Texas

Annie Merle Pulliam worked at Uvalde's Memorial Hospital during the fifties. During her off-hours she liked to look at the new babies in the nursery. One day she spied an unbelievably tiny infant. It was shriveled, with pinched and wizened features like those of a very old man. The poor little thing was all wrinkled and looked dried up. She shook her head and said, "Just look at that. Don't you tell me this drought isn't affecting everything in this county."

— Charles and Jane Willingham, Sabinal, Texas

R. J. and Ruth Rowden stuck to their dry-land farming techniques during the fifties, even when their neighbors began to put in irrigation systems. The neighbor's little boy thought R.J. was the all-around best guy and farmer in those parts and came down the road to see him every chance he got.

One morning in 1957, when the rains returned, the little boy's mother noticed how sad he seemed at the Sunday morning church service and asked him what was wrong.

"I bet Mr. Rowden isn't as happy about all this rain as other people seem to be."

"Why don't you think Mr. Rowden is happy?"

"Because he's a dry-land farmer, not a wet one."

— **Ruth Rowden, Wellman, Texas**

Worried schoolteachers in the fifties poked holes in the bottoms of tin cans and filled them with water to sprinkle the kids so they wouldn't panic the first time they saw rain.

— **Glenna Cavanaugh, Garland, Texas**

Near Christmas time a rookie teacher in a one-room schoolhouse in West Texas noticed that it had begun to snow outside. She called the class over to the window and exclaimed, "Look! It's snowing! Have you all ever seen snow before?"

The oldest boy in the class, who was about fifteen, replied politely, "No ma'am, but I seen it rain once't when I was little."

— Kevin McNelis, Arlington, Texas. There are numerous variations of this tale, which seems to be a particular favorite with people who were parents in the fifties.

On August 12, 1956, the doctor was preparing to break Norma Hughes' water and deliver her daughter. He said, "Well, let's see if we can't get some water for the Trinity River."

— Norma Hughes, Garland, Texas

A favorite practical joke played by youngsters in Midland during the fifties involved placing a phone call. Masquerading as a representative of the telephone company, the prankster would exlapin that due to the recent severe sandstorm a lot of their equipment had sand in it.

"We plan to blow out the lines with a burst of air, ma'am, and we don't want to make things worse for our customers who already have so much dust in their homes. If you will just set the phone down in a brown paper bag and secure it with a rubber band, that should catch the sand coming out of the line."

The trick then was to manage a look inside the victim's home to see if the phone was all done up. According to Charlene Walker Brazell, a lot of people fell for it, and she admits she could have been one of them.

— **Charlene Walker Brazell, Bartlesville, Oklahoma**

Weather Stories and Predictions

Two old men sat on the front porch one sweltering afternoon in 1953 discussing the drought. Rainfall in more than three-quarters of the state was well below normal, and dust bowl conditions had returned to parts of the Panhandle. Despite the grim reports, one of the men gazed hopefully at thunderclouds off in the east and said, "Joe, looks like rain, don't you think?"

"Sam, long as you've lived in West Texas you ought to know better'n that."

"But Joe, just look at those big clouds over there."

"Hell, Sam, they're just empties coming back from Florida."

— "Fine Wool and Clippings," *Sheep and Goat Raiser* (April 1953): 33

OR

". . . Naw, those are just empties coming back for another load of sand."

— Garry Baccus, Levelland, Texas

"I wish it would rain this summer until it's axle deep to a ferris wheel and snow this winter until it's downhill to Denver."

— Jerry Holmes, Plano, Texas

A weather watcher in Hereford, Texas, said to a reporter from the Clovis (New Mexico) *News-Journal*, "Heard you had two inches of rain in Clovis."

"We sure did. Why do you ask?"

"Well, shucks! If we'd have known you was going to have a good rain, we'd have come over and watched."

— Ken Francis, Abilene, Texas

"I wish it would rain six inches today, three inches tomorrow, two inches the next day, and settle down and rain an inch a day 'til it gets dry enough to plow."

— Jerry Holmes, Plano, Texas

In San Angelo, Texas, during the fifties a prankster seized the opportunity provided by wet cement on a sidewalk under repair on the east side of the Tom Green County Courthouse. The scamp pockmarked the surface and scrawled underneath, "See, it did rain here on May 8, 1956." Although Charles Haworth wasn't sure if he had recounted the date correctly, he said the drawing was still there years later.

— **Charles R. Haworth, Dallas, Texas**

In 1957 a rancher in Odessa called up his friend and said with elation, "The drought's broke, I've got proof!"

"What's your proof?"

"I saw a jack rabbit scoot across the road and there wasn't a rough-neck chasing him."

— **L. N. Davis, Boerne, Texas**

Real Estate and Business

In the summer of 1954, an Englishman visited Texas to buy a ranch. The real estate salesman could see that what he had to offer did not impress his client. As he drove along a rutted, dusty lane, a roadrunner jumped out of the brush and sprinted along in front of the truck. "My word, what is that?" asked the visitor.

The agent, hoping to salvage the sale, replied matter of factly, "That's the bird of paradise."

"Then he's a beastly long way from home," the Briton shot back.

— **Elmer Kelton, San Angelo, Texas**

One disgusted Texas farmer did manage to turn the real estate tables in his favor before quitting the state. As he and his family headed east after years of battling the harsh West Texas climate, a neighbor saw their wagon, pulled by an old mare and a scrawny ox, and flagged them down. "What happened to your other horse?" he asked.

"The drought got so bad ole Dollar just couldn't take it and he up and died on me. So I traded a feller two sections of land for this here ox," the farmer answered.

"Sounds like a steep trade," the neighbor remarked.

"I'm satisfied," he replied. "I offered him one section, but when we sat down to make out the papers, I found out the damned old fool couldn't read, so I made out the deed myself and stuck him with both sections."

— **Wallace O. Chariton,** *Texas Wit and Wisdom*, 37

A disgruntled Texas land developer said, "They told me we'd get twenty inches of rain a year. What they didn't tell me is it all came in one night."

— **Ken Francis, Abilene, Texas**

A disgusted rancher sold his place and told a friend, "Ever time I tried to drill a water well for my cattle, I kept hitting oil."

— **Dick Copeland, Garland, Texas**

Pete gave up and sold his "droughted out" ranch to someone who had more patience with the elements. Pete went to town and bought a hardware store. When his old friend Joe came in to see how Pete was doing with the new business, he picked up a hammer with a $1 price tag.

"That's not much for a hammer," Joe said. "What do you pay for 'em wholesale."

"Two dollars."

"Good Lord, Pete, you mean you lose a dollar every time you sell a hammer?"

"Yep, but it sure beats ranching."

— **John Fuller, Austin, Texas**

A stranger to West Texas bought a section of land sight unseen. When the real estate man took him out to see the parcel, it wasn't a pretty sight.

As the two men were standing surveying the scene, a prairie dog stuck his head out of his hole and looked them over.

"What kind of animal is that?" asked the new owner.

"That is a prairie dog," said the agent.

The stranger walked over to the hole, rolling up the deed to the land as he went. When he began stuffing the paper down the hole, the agent cried, "What are you doing?"

"If that little so-and-so can live in this country, he deserves to have the deed to it."

— **Katherine L. Hartgrove, San Angelo, Texas**

Did You Hear the One About...?

In 1951, a curious bystander watching a limping rancher working his sheep in a pen asked, "How'd you get crippled, old-timer?"

He replied, "Horse threw me out in the cedar brakes, broke my leg and run off."

Anxious to hear the rest of the story, the on-looker persisted. "How'd you get in to town?"

"Didn't. Crawled a mile or two and died."

"What do you mean you died? You're hobbling around here very much alive."

Slamming the gate behind the last skinny ewe, the man cocked an eye toward the sun, spat and asked, "You call this living?"

— "Is It Worth It?" *Sheep and Goat Raiser*
(December 1951): 41

During another drought in 1887 a man narrowly escaped a somewhat comical arrest in Anson. On a Monday morning passers-by spotted J. P. Cole walking down the street with a slicker draped over his arm. Since rain had not fallen in some time, this sight attracted considerable attention. S. C. Hines took offense as well as notice. He hastened to the sheriff's office and demanded the arrest of Cole. Hines claimed the charge should be "unlawfully carrying a slicker against the peace and dignity, dampness and future prospects of rain in the free state of Jones."

— **William C. Holden, "West Texas Droughts,"** *Southwestern Historical Quarterly* **32 (October 1928): 109**

Used to be that the difference between a rich West Texas sheepman and a poor one was that the poor one had to wash his own Cadillac. Not anymore. Now the wealthy one has enough water to wash a car.

— **"Fine Wool and Clippings,"** *Sheep and Goat Raiser* **(October 1951): 62**

Water got so scarce that one family used the same bath water every Saturday. They had to quit, though, after the time the quicksand almost got little brother on the last tub.

— **Ray Sperry, Idalou, Texas**

Old-timers used to say all West Texas lacked was water and good society. Since then they've drilled thousands of wells, built hundreds of dams, and shot dozens of tenderfeet, and the country still ain't no better off.

— "Foxtail Johnson Objects," *Sheep and Goat Raiser*
(December 1951): 53

Old-timers used to want Texas to have more water and good society. Nowadays we're only interested in important things. Give us water.

— "Foxtail Johnson Objects," *Sheep and Goat Raiser*
(March 1954:) 28

Used to be that cowmen and sheepmen shot each other on sight. This year, with prices being what they are, they've taken to shooting themselves.

— "Foxtail Johnson Objects," *Sheep and Goat Raiser*
(March 1954): 28

"I made a bet with three other fellers that it never will rain again."
"Sounds like a bad bet to me."
"I don't know. Two of them have paid off."

— Ray Sperry, Idalou, Texas; This is one of the most popular drought jokes I've received. More than a dozen people sent it in. Many thanks to each of you.

In 1954 a cowboy complained about how rough his job was getting, "With all this feedin' all you gotta do to round up is ride out in the middle of a pasture, honk the horn, and get out of the way when the cows come running."

— Cartoon, *Sheep and Goat Raiser*
(March 1954): 25

One night in 1955 Abner M. Ussery, Jr., of Blessing, Texas, came home from a late session of building fence. While unloading his tools, he accidentally dragged a chain out of the back of his pick-up. It fell to the ground and down a crack.

"This is hog wallow country," said Abner, "and the cracks in the ground are unreal." Since it was dark, he couldn't see to retrieve the chain. The next morning he went outside, got down on all fours, and looked in the crack. "I couldn't see it, but I heard something. I put my ear to the ground, and sure enough, it was still falling."

— Abner M. Ussery, Jr., Blessing, Texas

OR

Johnnie K. Spuriell swore to his wife that during the fifties drought he fell into a crack in the ground on his farm five miles from Coolidge and had to crawl all the way to town to get out.

— Ollene Spuriell, Hubbard, Texas

A farmer north of Big Spring had the good luck to have a good oil well completed on his farm right in the middle of the fifties drought. When he told a neighbor he wished the drillers would go ahead and sink another well, the neighbor said, "Why, isn't this one enough to make you a good living?"

"Oh sure," said the man, "but I'd like to farm too."

— **Juil E. Reid, Stanton, Texas**

Farmers used to gather at the gin office in Flomot to talk about their crops and the weather. Grady always got more rain than anyone else in Motley County and liked to brag about the worth of his crop and how much he'd get for it — until the day he stalked out in a huff when a fellow farmer said: "Grady, I can't afford to buy your crop this morning at that price, but I am prepared to give you $350 for that rain gauge of yours."

— **Ray Sperry, Idalou, Texas**

After a long dry spell, it finally rained. A curious Texan sent the stuff in to a laboratory to be analyzed. The report came back, "Twenty percent moisture."

— **Charles Wilkinson, Anson, Texas**

OR

Some cafes in the fifties started serving two glasses of water to each customer since the stuff was only 50 percent moisture at best.

— **M.E. Kite, Fritch, Texas**

During the 1950s a tractor factory marketed a special "drought model." With no seat or steering wheel, it was designed for the farmer who had lost his ass and didn't know which way to go.

— **Juil E. Reid, Stanton, Texas**

During the fifties a local rancher appeared in town one day driving a brand new Cadillac.

"What gives?" demanded one of his friends, standing by his beat-up old truck. "I can't hardly afford gas for this ole piece of junk."

"Well," said the rancher, "you know all them feed sacks been stacking up behind my barn? Well, I sold 'em and bought this here car."

— **John Winslow, Menard,**
and G. Strange, Colorado City, Texas

A farmer cut down some trees and used the logs to build a pen for his cows just before a drought set in. Day after day in the baking sun, those logs dried out until it looked like the corral would fall apart just any day.

One night the farmer was delighted to be awakened by the sound of rain. He rolled over and went back to sleep, thinking about better times, but the next morning when he went out to feed the cows, he found those thirsty logs had swollen up and strangled those poor animals.

— **Mrs. Martha DeSpain, Marble Falls, Texas**

In the fifties, the South Texas regional sales manager for a firm dependent on the farm-and-ranch trade asked his salesmen to stand up and offer their personal assurance they would meet their sales quotas across the board.

There was a deadly silence. Finally, a man from Laredo could stand it no longer. "One of you bastards say something!" he roared.

— **Bill Low, Dallas, Texas**

After a good rain that put his drought-stricken ranch "knee deep in grass," an old-timer went into town for a shave. The barber charged him only two bits instead of the usual three because his face wasn't as long as it used to be.

— **Bruce C. Faulkner, Tyler, Texas**

Outside Snyder, some wag changed the town's welcoming sign during the fifties from, "Welcome to Snyder, Texas where oil flows and cotton grows," to "Welcome to Snyder, Texas, where sand flies and cotton dies and the rent's too damn high."

— **Herman Bond, Cedar Hill, Texas**

At the end of the fifties drought three farmers managed to sell their cotton and bought a jug to celebrate. After a few rounds, one said, "Now that the drought's broke, I'm gonna buy my wife a new kitchen stove."

"I'm gonna buy my wife a new refrigerator."

The third man spoke up and said, "Give me the jug. I ain't out of debt yet."

— **Paul Bishop, Big Spring, Texas**

The Extremes

A typical tall-tale designed to make light of changeable Texas weather featured a cowboy riding along in blistering summer heat "hotter'n Satan in long handles." He turned around to find a "blizzard whizzin' in" just behind him. Putting the spurs to his horse the cowboy tried to outrun the snow storm. When he reached the barn back at the ranch and began to unsaddle his horse, he discovered something peculiar about the animal. "Danged if . . . [he] didn't find its forequarters plum' foamy with sweat and its hindquarters frozen solid with ice . . ."

— J. Frank Dobie, *The Flavor of Texas*, as quoted by Stan Hoig, *The Humor of the American Cowboy*, 40

A story on the Associated Press wire for April 9, 1952, reported two days' worth of Texas weather.

Tuesday it was 98 at Childress, the hottest in the nation. Wednesday morning it was below freezing at Dalhart and snowing. At mid-

38

morning the Dallas U.S. Weather Bureau warned Texans to watch out for tornadoes. A half hour later several parts of the state were rocked by earth tremors.

— Quoted in John Edward Weems, *"If You Don't Like the Weather . . .,"* 26

A tourist remarked to a native Texan: "Awfully rainy weather, just like the Flood."

The cowboy frowned and asked, "The Flood?"

"You know," said the stranger, "the Flood, Noah, the Ark, Mount Ararat."

The cowboy shook his head, "Sorry, friend, but I ain't seen the paper yet this morning."

— Boyce House, *I Give You Texas*, 7

Mrs. Leo Bishop lived thirty-five miles northeast of Del Rio in the 1950s. When she heard a version of this joke to the effect that when it rained forty days and forty nights West Texas just got a quarter of an inch, she remarked, "Well, it laid the dust out here."

— Bettye Robbins, Jasper, Texas

One afternoon in 1957, two Bandera men sweated over the chore of building a water-gap in a dry creek bed. Suddenly, a clap of thunder sounded and pelting raindrops drove them to the shelter of a large cedar bush on the bank. No sooner had they reached its branches than a four-foot wall of water roared across the spot where they had been standing.

One man turned to the other and said, "By damn this Texas sure is a funny world, ain't it? It's either too 'nuff or too nuthin' in all the wrong places."

— Quoted in Thomas M. Hatfield, "Drought and Texas Cities," *West Texas Historical Association Yearbook* 40 (October 1964): 40

George H. Cox built a ranch house halfway between Eden and Paint Rock in Concho County in 1908. He raised sheep and some mules for the army, but had no water on his land. He often took a wagon load of barrels to the Concho River ten miles to the north to haul back water.

On one trip, the sky darkened and let loose a "helluva rain." George stopped in downtown Paint Rock to wait out the worst of the storm. He could barely contain his excitement. He dumped the barrels in the street and took off for home, whooping and hollering like a crazy man with the townfolk cheering him on.

But when he got back to the ranch, he found that it hadn't even sprinkled enough there to settle the dust. Red-faced he returned, collected his barrels, and headed for the Concho.

— Margaret A. Cox, Austin, Texas

In the thirties a newspaperman couldn't decide if long-awaited rains that broke a drought but claimed several lives were good or bad. The headline he composed read, "Beneficial rains cause ten deaths in West Texas."

— House, *I Give You Texas*, 6

A Northerner was persuaded to invest in Texas land when he grew tired of snow and ice. Around the first of November, he asked a Mexican ranch hand, "Juan, have you ever seen snow here?"

"No, señor," Juan answered, "but I have seen rain — twice."

— Elmer Kelton, *The Time It Never Rained*

Driving through the barren West Texas landscape in the fifties, a Yankee stopped and asked for directions and was told, "You take this road straight west for eighty-three miles to the tree, where you turn south."

— F.N. (Doc) Carter, San Angelo, Texas

It hadn't rained in a long time. An old farmer and his wife were sitting out on the porch one night and he heard a solitary croaking down by the dry lake.

"Do you hear that blessed little frog calling for rain?" he asked his wife. "Maybe he can call some up for us. We're getting desperate."

Well, the next day it commenced to raining as if it would never stop. The streams spilled over their banks. The fields flooded. The livestock was stranded. Everything was in a mess.

Again the farmer and his wife sat out on the porch watching the downpour and listening to millions of frogs croaking down at the lake.

The wife said something that her husband didn't hear. She repeated herself, but he still didn't catch it and snapped, "I can't hear anything on account of those damn frogs."

— **Ray Sperry, Idalou, Texas**

In Hockley County near Anton, Texas, the farm known as the Loper Place seemed cursed by a lack of rain. One day in 1956 the current owner was talking to his neighbor about how frustrating it was to see the rest of the area get a good shower when none ever fell on his land.

The neighbor sadly explained that the farm used to be part of the Spade Ranch. "They say that when the cowboys were caught out in a thunderstorm on horseback, they'd head to the Loper Place to dry off."

— **Garry Baccus, Levelland, Texas**

An Easterner was driving through Pecos when he stopped and asked a local, "How much rain do you get a year?"

"About eight inches."

"That's not very much."

"Yeah, but you ought to be here on the day we get it."

— F.N. (Doc) Carter, San Angelo, Texas

A West Texas rancher called on Austin for drought relief. The agent at the state office advised him that he was not entitled to receive any government aid.

"Why in the hell not?" he demanded.

"Because your county has received in excess of fourteen inches of rain this year," the agent replied stiffly.

"That's true," snapped the rancher, "and I vividly remember the exact day it happened."

— Alfred B. Blackard, Mineral Wells, Texas

A West Texas rancher stood with Noah surveying the Flood. "Well," he said, "it's a pretty good rain and if we could get another one like it in about ten days, we would be doing all right."

— Elsie Adele Queen, Dallas, Texas

A New York Yankee drove through Langtry, Texas, one hot summer day in the 1950s. As he neared the outskirts of town, he noticed a man who looked like he was casting for fish, but he had no fishing pole. Not to mention that Langtry, Texas, was dry as the heart of a standstorm at mid-day in hell. No water in sight for a hundred miles.

The Yankee turned the car around and rushed back into town. He dashed over to the local jail, where he found the sheriff leaning on a hitching post chewing tobacco.

Out of breath, the Yankee said, "Sheriff, there's a crazy man outside of town casting for fish and he has no pole and no water. You have to go pick him up, quick!"

The sheriff reached down, grabbed a hand full of air, jerked up his hand several times and said, "I will, soon as I get this damn motor boat started."

— **Larry Howard, Dallas, Texas**

Dust and Wind

In the Panhandle, where dust storms in 1954 and 1955 invoked memories of the "Dirty Thirties," a motorist carefully followed the tail lights of a pick-up for an hour until they abruptly stopped. Before he could brake, he slammed into the truck.

"Why in the devil don't you put out your hand when you're going to stop?" he yelled out the window.

"Why should I?" asked the other driver, "I'm in my own sheep barn."

— **"Fine Wool and Clippings,"** *Sheep and Goat Raiser*
(March 1953): 49

A visitor from back east, exasperated by the dry, dusty wind in West Texas, asked a local, "Is it always like this?"

"Nope," the ranchman answered, "it's usually worse."

— **"Fine Wool and Clippings,"** *Sheep and Goat Raiser*
(April 1953): 33

One Texan claimed that during the fifties the dust storms got so bad and the prairie dogs so confused that the poor little critters were digging-in three feet above the ground.

— **Claudia Kolar, Seadrift, Texas**

In the thirties a farm wife grew so weary of fighting the dust storms that she served her family's dinners under the tablecloth. After the blessing, each person raised the edge of the cloth, ducked under, and started to eat.

— **Matthew Paul Bonnifield,** *The Dust Bowl,* **191**

During a dry summer in the mid-1980s, Charles Wilkinson and his wife, Jean, were driving by Lake Phantom near Abilene. The lake was pretty low and Charles noticed a cloud hanging over it. Moving closer, he realized it was dust being kicked up by the fish swimming to the deep end.

— **Charles Wilkinson, Anson, Texas**

The Borger area suffered through two terrible dust storms in the spring of 1953. During the first storm it got so dark the streetlights came on at midday and the wind tore sheet metal roofs off their moorings. During the peak of the second storm it began to rain — mud. Shortly after the storms, a local employee asked for a leave of absence citing his wife's need for time in a drier climate. The request was denied so the fellow resigned and moved to Albuquerque.

— **D.M. Poundstone, Fort Worth, Texas**

Dust swirled knee-deep around the farm house in the thirties. It hadn't rained in years, and Papa was going off his rocker. Every night he dragged the whole family out to the yard to kneel in the dust and pray for rain.

One night during this ritual, a cloud appeared on the horizon and Papa began to call out to it, "Come over here! Come over here!" The cloud start coming, growing bigger and blacker by the minute until a funnel cloud erupted from its midst and dipped to the ground.

Sending Mama and the kids to the cellar, Papa stood his ground and changed his tune. "Go around! Go around!" he yelled at the sky. When the family came out, Papa and the house stood firm, but the dust was still there.

— **Mrs. Hazel Taylor, Eastland, Texas**

During a Panhandle dust storm in the fifties, M.E. Kite looked out his kitchen window and saw two prairie dogs digging furiously — ten feet off the ground.

— **M.E. Kite, Fritch, Texas**

A raccoon was startled to find a prairie dog on the limb beside him.

"What are you doing in my tree?" he asked.

The befuddled prairie dog answered, "Danged if I know. I was five feet down a new hole when the wind stopped."

— **Dick Copeland, Garland, Texas**

A rancher decided to fence a section of his Sutton County ranch. Before he was finished, the wind stopped blowing and he found himself sinking a post-hole 5,000 feet in the air over Big Bend.

— **Dick Copeland, Garland, Texas**

An old rancher reached the end of his financial rope and went to the bank to get a loan on his place.

"I'll have to survey it," said the banker.

Looking out the window at the dust clouds rolling down the street, the rancher said, "Don't bother, son. Here it comes now."

— **Dick Copeland, Garland, Texas**

A passenger on a train was chugging through a West Texas dust storm. Suddenly, he looked out the window and saw a "cat skinner" on a D8 Cat with a dozer blade, twelve feet in the air, trying to bulldoze himself back down to the ground.

— R.W. Wing, Lewisville, Texas

"Sure does look dry," said the old-timer to his uncle. "All the clods have gone to powder. This land's just worthless."

"Naw," answered the uncle, "it's just dry on top. Underneath, the part they tax, is still worth plenty, and I've got the overdue tax notices to prove it."

— John Igo, San Antonio, Texas

During one of the worst days of the thirties' Dust Bowl, Ebb Dickerson struggled down Wall Street in Midland, Texas. A band of on-lookers in the Midland National Bank watched him holding onto his hat and trying to walk at the same time.

Ebb finally made it into the bank, with the wind sending paper flying as he opened the door.

"Hey, Ebb," called out a jokester, "how's the weather out there?"

"Well," said Ebb, "if I owed a feller a sand storm and he wouldn't take this one, I'll be durned if I'd pay him."

— Grace LeMonds, Lubbock, Texas

The Drought Novel

Texan novelist Elmer Kelton displayed a fine perception of the presence and value of dark, gallows humor in his novel *The Time It Never Rained*, a classic account of the seven-year drought of the 1950s.

In the 1930s, Kelton watched his father battle the nagging lack of rain on the McElroy ranch near Crane. The 1950s found Kelton working as a reporter and livestock editor for the *San Angelo Standard Times*. In *The Time It Never Rained*, he presents a portrait of the demoralizing effects of drought through the losing struggle of his main character, rancher Charlie Flagg.[1]

As Flagg and his neighbors suffer increasingly from the drought, a ranch hand, Lupe, dredges up an age-worn joke, in a vain effort to comfort his employer. "The time Old Noah built his Ark, we don't get but a quarter-inch here at Rio Seco." And when the braggart Rounder Pike assembles an audience, he relates the unhappy fate of the San Angelo cow thief who turned himself in after he stole two heifers and lost $80 on the deal.[2]

In 1987, Kelton observed that the jokes circulating in the 1950s were a way of helping people get by a day at a time. Something had to offset the brutal conditions in people's minds. Kelton remembered San Angelo dust storms that turned the sun into a muddy orange ball. He saw bawling cattle follow pickups through pastures as stockmen tossed government feed off the tailgates. And he recorded an exchange between a Big Spring banker and his client. "If it don't rain pretty soon, looks like I'm gonna have to rob a bank," said the executive.

"If it don't rain pretty soon," replied the rancher, "looks like I've already robbed a bank."[3]

The Drought Cartoon

Drought humor gained a visual dimension in the 1950s in the work of Texan cartoonist Ace Reid, who grew up in Wichita County in the 1930s. His father, an oil field worker and small ranch operator, waged a daily battle against triple enemies: drought, depression, and Dust Bowl. This struggle left indelible images in the younger Reid's mind and gave him the determination to make a better life for himself. He did not foresee, however, that the key to realizing that dream would be a combination of artistic ability and the one thing he hoped to escape — drought.[1]

After returning from the South Pacific when World War II ended and attempting various business ventures, Reid sent in his first cartoon, which appeared in the *National Quarter Horse Journal* in 1946. By 1951 his drawings appeared regularly in the *West Texas Livestock Weekly*, just as the opening stages of the seven-year drought became apparent. Reid, a colorful folk figure in his own right, used his "Cowpokes" panel and the laconic ranch hands, Jake and Zeb, to depict the ironies and hardships of life in drought-stricken Texas.[2]

The theme proved so successful, Reid continued

52

to use it long after the rains returned in 1957. In 1966 his cowpokes read a newspaper whose headlines proclaimed, "Drouth Gets Worse," "Cattle Prices Hit Bottom," and "Feed Yards Go Broke." Jake's comment: "Them people in that poverty area are livin' on $400 a year. That beats me by about $200." That same year, Jake visited a fortune teller and commented, "Madame, that blond sounds fine, but can't you be more definite about the cow market and the next rain?"[3]

His attitude ran true to form in 1974. With a spraying rig strapped to his back, Jake told Zeb, "Naw, I ain't tryin' to kill my bitter weeds. It's so dry I'm goin' down and spray my fish fer ticks!"[4] In another panel he blasted the myth of the land-rich Texan. "To think, all this ranch is mine, 15,000 acres of land, no grass, five miles of creek, and no water."[5]

In spring 1990, when areas around Sanderson and Dryden measured only two inches of rainfall in two years, the boys were shown on the loading dock of Bud's Feed Store. As Jake dragged a feed sack into the truck, he said, "Yeah, we jist got over one drought, now we're gittin' ready fer another one." That summer Jake surveyed his cattle and explained, "Now this is my welfare herd. They jist stand around and bawl for another handout."[6]

Notes

Preface

1. Dean Chenoweth and Elmer Kelton, "Texas Dry Humor," *Reader's Digest* (March 1953): 71-72.

2. "Farms Dry Up Again — But Farmers Stay Put," *Business Weekly* (22 May 1954): 134; Robert L. Lowry, *A Study of Droughts in Texas* (Austin: Texas Board of Water Engineers, 1959), 13-18; *Texas Business Review* 24, no. 4 (April 1951):8.

3. Gwyn Prins, "Oral History" in *New Perspectives on Historical Writing* (University Park, Pennsylvania: The Pennsylvania State University Press, 1991), 120; Barbara Allen, "Story in Oral History: Clues to Historical Consciousness." *The Journal of American History* (September 1992): 611.

4. Albert Rapp, *The Origins of Wit and Humor* (New York: E.P. Dutton and Co, Inc., 1951), 167; Chenoweth and Kelton, "Texas Dry Humor," *Reader's Digest* (March 1953): 71-72.

5. "Fine Wool and Clippings," *Sheep and Goat Raiser* (October 1950): 56 and (August 1953): 58; quoted in William C. Holden, "West Texas Droughts," *Southwestern Historical Quarterly* 32 (October 1928): 109.

6. Avner Ziv, *Personality and Sense of Humor* (New York: Springer Publishing Company, 1984), 51-53; Rapp, *The Origins of Wit and Humor*, 167, 169.

7. Lawrence E. Mintz, "American Humour and the Spirit of the Times," in Anthony J. Chapman and Hugh C. Foot, eds. *It's A Funny Thing, Humour* (New York: Pergamon Press, 1977), 17.

8. Ziv, *Personality and Sense of Humor*, 55.

9. Ace Reid, interview by Rana K. Williamson, Kerrville, Texas, 31 October 1987, hereafter cited as Reid interview; U.S. Department of Agriculture, *Texas Historic Livestock Statistics, 1867-1985*, 5, 45, 51. Overall livestock production figures for the period 1951 to 1958 show marked declines in the value of cattle and sheep production but only a slight dip and then a considerable climb in mohair production from 1954 to 1957.

10. Walter Prescott Webb, "Billion-Dollar Cure for Texas Drought," *Harper's* (December 1953): 73; John R. Erickson, *Ace Reid-Cowpoke* (Perryton, Texas: Maverick Books, 1984), 146; J. Frank Dobie, *The Flavor of Texas*, as quoted by Stan Hoig, *The Humor of the American Cowboy* (Lincoln: University of Nebraska Press, 1958): 40.

11. John T. Carr, *Texas Droughts: Causes and Prediction* (Austin: Texas Water Development Board, 1966), 4; *The Texas Almanac, 1961-62* ed. s.v. "Texas Annual Average Precipitation" (Dallas: The Belo Corporation); Chenoweth and Kelton, "Texas Dry Humor," *Reader's Digest* (March 1953): 72. The following series of precipitation averages include two years prior and one year after the seven-year drought: 1949 — 34.34, 1950 — 25.17, 1951 — 21.09, 1952 — 22.94, 1953 — 23.72, 1954 — 18.30, 1955 — 22.85, 1956 — 16.20, 1957 — 36.93, 1958 — 32.71 and 1959 — 31.29.

The Drought Novel

1. Kelton interview; Kelton, *The Time It Never Rained*.

2. Kelton, *The Time It Never Rained*, 114, 232.

3. Kelton interview; Chenoweth and Kelton, "Texas Dry Humor," 71-72.

The Drought Cartoon

1. John R. Erickson, *Ace Reid-Cowpoke* (Perryton, Texas: Maverick Books, 1984), 31; Reid interview.

2. Ibid.; In marketing his cartoons, Reid worked at developing a public image that kept his name in the news. He took his lead from the silent film star Tom Mix, who reportedly made his entrances with the challenge, "Bring on the whiskey and the women."

Reid, with the help of a group of friends including Slim Pickens and Hondo Crouch, became a flamboyant figure. For instance, he once rented a hotel room for an armadillo that accompanied him to a speaking engagement. On another occasion Reid forged President Lyndon B. Johnson's signature on a men's room wall. The forgery was so convincing that the owner of the establishment proudly preserved it under glass.

3. Ace Reid, *Ace Reid's Cowpokes Comin' Yore Way* (Kerrville, Texas: Ace Reid Enterprises, Inc., 1966), n.p.

4. Ace Reid, *Ace Reid's Cowpokes Ride Again* (Kerrville, Texas: Ace Reid Cowpokes, Inc., 1974), n.p.

5. Ibid.

6. Joe McClure, "Western Drought — Trans-Pecos Region Suffering Deeply From Two Year Dry Spell," *San Angelo Standard Times*, 1 April 1990, 1, 4A; Ace Reid, "Cowpokes," *San Marcos News*, 29 March 1990, 4; "Cowpokes," *Junction Eagle*, 7 June 1990.